LEVEL

3

Fact Reader

Mythical Beasts

100 FUN Facts About Real Animals and the Myths They Inspire

Stephanie Warren Drimmer

NATIONAL GEOGRAPHIC

Washington, D.C.

For Hailey, Ella, Connor, Jack, and Oliver —S.W.D.

Published by National Geographic Partners, LLC, Washington, DC 20036.

Designed by Design Superette

Author's Note
Do you love unicorns and dragons? Legends from around the world are filled with tales of mythical creatures. But unbelievable animals aren't just the stuff of stories: Some are incredibly real. Some animals even inspired the myths! In this book, you'll read about real-life amazing creatures and the myths they inspired.

Publisher's Note
The cover photo features a green dragon sculpture at a Chinese temple and a venomous hairy bush viper snake. The title page has a bird of paradise sitting on a branch, and the table of contents shows a Chinese golden dragon statue.

The author and publisher gratefully acknowledge the fact-checking review of this book by Michelle Harris, and the literacy review of this book by Mariam Jean Dreher, professor emerita of reading education, University of Maryland, College Park.

Photo Credits
Abbreviations: AL = Alamy Stock Photo; AS = Adobe Stock; GI = Getty Images; MP = Minden Pictures; NGIC = National Geographic Image Collection; NP = Nature Picture Library; SS = Shutterstock
Cover: (UP), dangdumrong/GI; (LO), Mark Kostich/AS; header (THROUGHOUT), Gluiki/AS; 1, Tim Laman/NGIC; 3, seaskylab/SS; 4 (UP), tristan tan/SS; 4 (CTR & LO), storm/AS; 5 (UP LE), Mike Floyd/Daily Mail/SS; 5 (UP CTR), Paulo Oliveira/AL; 5 (UP RT), Vishnevskiy Vasily/SS; 5 (LO LE), pathdoc/AS; 5 (LO RT), MichaelTaylor3d/SS; 6-7, danielegay/AS; 8, Gift of John D. Rockefeller Jr., 1937/Metropolitan Museum of Art; 9, Flip Nicklin/MP; 10, Classic Image/AL; 11, James R. White/AS; 12, Daniel/AS; 13, Historia/SS; 14 (UP), Kim Steele/GI; 14 (LO), Charles R. Knight/NGIC; 15 (UP), bigjom/AS; 15 (CTR), Hilary Andrews/NG Staff; 15 (LO), Franco Tempesta; 16, Marc Dozier/GI; 17, blue-sea.cz/SS; 18, llaurent789/AS; 19 (UP LE), mojoeks/SS; 19 (UP RT), Archivist/AS; 19 (LO), DeAgostini/GI; 20 (UP), PIXATERRA/AS; 20 (LO), Yellow Cat/SS; 21 (UP), Pedro/AS; 21 (CTR), Hamilton/AS; 21 (LO), manfredxy/AS; 22 (UP), Zacarias da Mata/AS; 22 (LO), imageBROKER/AS; 23 (LE), Joel Sartore/NGIC; 23 (RT), James/AS; 24-25, Paulo de Oliveira/MP; 25 (UP), dezignor/SS; 25 (LO), jorisvo/AS; 26, Stephen Dalton/MP; 27 (UP), Photo Researchers/Science History Images/AL; 27 (LO), Werner Forman Archive/Museum fur Volkerkunde, Berlin/Heritage Images/AL; 28, Artville; 29, Simon Litten/AL; 30, Nicholas Smythe/Science Source; 31 (UP), Tier Und Naturfotografie J und C Sohns/GI; 31 (CTR), David Shale/NP; 31 (LO), Sahara Frost/AS; 32-33, Bence Mate/NP; 33, vchalup/AS; 34, Jagoush/SS; 35 (UP), SciePro/SS; 35 (LO), Yiming Chen/GI; 36 (UP), The History Collection/AL; 36 (LO), johnandersonphoto/GI; 36-37, Thorsten Negro/GI; 37, Marcus Lelle/500px/GI; 38 (UP), Photo Researchers/Science History Images/AL; 38 (LO), Kazakova Maryia/AS; 39 (UP), Matt Jeppson/SS; 39 (INSET), BBC Natural History/GI; 39 (LO), Oliver Thompson-Holmes/AL; 40 (UP), Satoshi Kuribayashi/MP; 40 (LO), Chien Lee/MP; 41, Martin Harvey/AL; 42-43, Michael Lynch/SS; 44 (UP LE), Gift of Mrs. Myron C. Taylor, 1938/Metropolitan Museum of Art; 44 (UP RT), GlobalP/GI; 44 (CTR), Stan/AS; 44-45 (LO), Eric Isselée/AS; 45 (LE), warpaintcobra/AS; 45 (CTR), Tim Flach/GI; 45 (RT), Purchase, Lila Acheson Wallace Gift, 1972/Metropolitan Museum of Art

Library of Congress Cataloging-in-Publication Data
Names: Drimmer, Stephanie Warren, author.
Title: Mythical beasts. (Level 3) : 100 fun facts about real animals and the myths they inspire / Stephanie Warren Drimmer.
Description: Washington, D.C. : National Geographic Kids, 2022. | Series: National geographic readers | Includes index. | Audience: Ages 6-9 | Audience: Grades 2-3
Identifiers: LCCN 2019055273 (print) | LCCN 2019055274 (ebook) | ISBN 9781426338939 (paperback) | ISBN 9781426338946 (library binding) | ISBN 9781426338953 (ebook)
Subjects: LCSH: Animals, Mythical--Juvenile literature. | Legends--Juvenile literature.
Classification: LCC GR825 .D75 2022 (print) | LCC GR825 (ebook) | DDC 398.24/54--dc23
LC record available at https://lccn.loc.gov/2019055273
LC ebook record available at https://lccn.loc.gov/2019055274

Printed in the United States of America
22/WOR/2

Contents

1

The Baku, a mythical Chinese and Japanese creature that eats dreams, could have been inspired by the tapir, a real animal that looks like a pig with a long snout.

2

Australian Aboriginals told of a monster called the bunyip. Experts now believe that the myth may have been based on a now extinct animal called *Diprotodon*.

3

Like the "trickster" character Coyote of Native American myths, real coyotes are known to be smart and curious.

4

Many ancient people thought unicorns were real animals. The myth may have been based on a sighting of an Indian rhinoceros.

5

Birds called swifts can stay airborne without landing for 10 months straight.

6

The basilisk was an enormous mythical snake. *Titanoboa* was a real monster-size snake as long as a city bus. It lived 60 million years ago.

7

Stories in ancient Greek mythology featured a giant monster with 100 hands. One species of millipede has even more limbs: 750!

8

In Arabic folklore, the Roc was a bird that could pick up and eat a human. Fossils show that long ago, large birds really did prey on people.

9

Humans have long been fascinated by horses: They inspired many mythical creatures such as centaurs, unicorns, and Pegasus (shown here).

25 COOL FACTS

ABOUT **MYTHICAL BEASTS**

AND UNBELIEVABLE **REAL-LIFE CREATURES**

10
Dolphins sleep with one eye open! This feat helps them watch for danger even while resting.

11
Wood frogs can survive being frozen in the winter. In the spring, they thaw out and hop away.

12
DNA testing has found that most hair samples that people claimed had come from the mythical yeti actually belonged to bears.

13
When scientists discovered the fossil of a prehistoric whale that was 50 feet long, they named it Leviathan, after a biblical sea monster.

14
Myths of giant sea serpents might have been inspired by the real-life giant oarfish, which can grow to be more than 50 feet long.

15
In legends, the Mongolian death worm can kill by zapping its victims with electricity—just like an electric eel.

16
A real-life Bigfoot existed until 100,000 years ago! This giant ape, called *Gigantopithecus,* stood more than 10 feet tall.

17
The mythical Nemean lion had a hide so tough no weapons could cut it. Alligators have bony plates that make them almost as tough.

18
The snapping shrimp has a power that seems supernatural: When it closes a claw, it sends out a jet of water at nearly 100 feet a second.

19
Fenrir, a mythical Norse wolf, was said to be so strong even the gods couldn't tame him. Real-life wolves are so strong their jaws can crush bones.

20
The ancient Greeks believed that half-woman, half-bird creatures called sirens could trick sailors into crashing their ships.

21
Some people think the legendary Loch Ness monster is a plesiosaur—a type of sea-dwelling reptile. Scientists say plesiosaurs went extinct about 66 million years ago.

22
The mythical Greek monster called the Minotaur had the body of a human and the head and tail of a bull.

23
In ancient Egypt, cats were thought to be magical creatures that could bring good luck to their owners.

24
Lenape and Iroquois (IR-uh-kwoy) legends tell that the world was created on the back of a giant sea turtle.

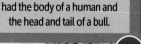

25
According to Chinese myth, all the animals of the world raced to see which 12 would become the symbols of the zodiac.

Introduction

People once believed the world was full of dragons, unicorns, and other mythical creatures.

These animals weren't real. But fantastic beasts really do share our planet. Some were once mistaken for legendary animals. Others are so strange they don't look real. And still others have abilities so extraordinary they seem impossible. Let's meet some mythical beasts and amazing real-life creatures!

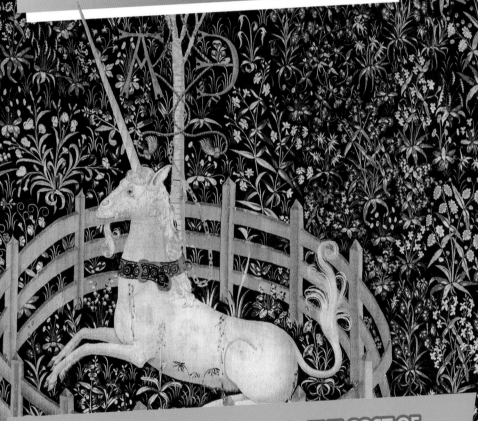

CHAPTER 1

Mistaken Identities

Queen Elizabeth I paid £10,000—THE COST OF AN ENTIRE CASTLE at the time—for what she thought was a unicorn's horn covered with jewels.

Vikings once collected enormous horns that washed up on northern beaches near Arctic waters. Then, they would sell them to people who believed they came from unicorns.

But the "horns" were actually the tusks of narwhals, animals that live in the frigid waters of the Arctic. To this day, narwhals are often called the unicorns of the sea. In fact, they are one of many animals that have been mistaken for mythical creatures.

The tusk is actually A TOOTH THAT GROWS OUT of the animals' upper lip.

A narwhal's tusk CAN BE NEARLY NINE FEET LONG.

Scientists aren't sure what narwhals USE THEIR TUSKS FOR.

illustration of Henry Hudson's ship

In 1608, explorer Henry Hudson wrote that a few of his crew saw a creature with THE BODY OF A WOMAN AND THE TAIL OF A PORPOISE swimming alongside his ship.

People have been reporting mermaid sightings for centuries. But experts believe that the strange swimmers were actually manatees.

These sea creatures have fish-like tails but can turn their heads from side to side, like humans. Sometimes, they even stand on their tails in shallow water, with their upper bodies above the surface. That makes them look like people cooling off in the ocean. It's no wonder explorers got confused!

Manatees are DISTANTLY RELATED TO ELEPHANTS.

A manatee relative is the dugong, which gets its name from the Malay word for "LADY OF THE SEA."

In 1853, an enormous creature with long tentacles was found stranded on a beach in Denmark. IT LOOKED LIKE A SEA MONSTER!

illustration of the mythical kraken

Ancient sailors told tales of a terrible sea monster called the kraken. They said it could pull entire ships underwater and swallow the whole crew! But experts believe the mythical kraken was based on sightings of giant squid.

illustration of a giant squid found stranded on a beach in Newfoundland

Like all squid, giant squid have **THREE HEARTS.**

Giant squid have EYES THE SIZE OF DINNER PLATES.

The real-life animal isn't dangerous to humans, but it is fierce: Giant squid can be as long as a city bus—and they do battle with whales!

In the past, people thought the bones of some ancient animals belonged to mythical creatures.

DRAGONS: When ancient people found dinosaur fossils, they didn't realize the animals had been extinct for millions of years. Instead, they looked at dinosaurs' big teeth, long tails, and claws and thought the bones came from living dragons.

GRIFFINS: Some experts think the legendary griffin—a half-eagle, half-lion creature—came from fossil discoveries of *Protoceratops*. These dinosaurs had four legs and enormous beaks.

CYCLOPES: Greek mythology told of a one-eyed giant called a cyclops (SY-klops). But once, on the Greek island of Crete, real giants roamed: now extinct relatives of the elephant! The animal's skull had a large opening in the center for the trunk. The ancient Greeks may have thought the hole was for one eye, and that the skull belonged to a cyclops!

"Cyclops" means "ROUND EYE."

a *Basilosaurus* skeleton

SEA SERPENTS: In 1834, the remains of a "sea monster" were discovered in Alabama, U.S.A. Later, scientists found that the bones really belonged to an ancient whale that lived 40 million years ago. Called *Basilosaurus*, it was about 65 feet long—longer than a semitruck.

CHAPTER 2

Too Strange to Believe

Aboriginal painting of a rainbow serpent

In Australian Aboriginal legend, the RAINBOW SERPENT WAS AN IMMORTAL CREATURE with a multicolored body.

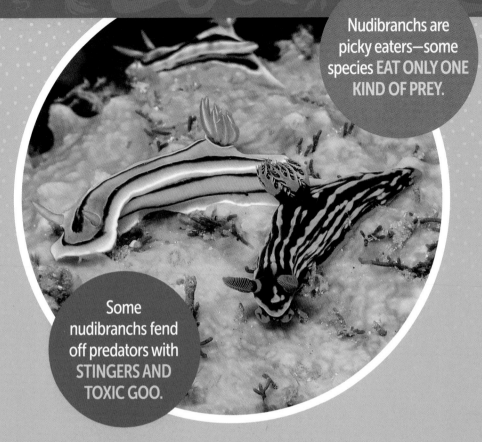

Nudibranchs are picky eaters—some species EAT ONLY ONE KIND OF PREY.

Some nudibranchs fend off predators with STINGERS AND TOXIC GOO.

A rainbow-colored beast sounds like it could only come from a story. But nudibranchs (NEW-dih-branks) live throughout the world's oceans and come in every color combination imaginable. They get their bright colors from the foods they eat, such as corals and anemones.

Like the nudibranch, some real-life animals are so strange looking, they hardly look real!

The horselike okapi (oh-KAH-pee) is so hard to find in the wild that it was once THOUGHT TO BE A UNICORN.

Okapis are related to giraffes—but they have the body of a horse and the stripes of a zebra. They are shy creatures that live in the African rainforest.

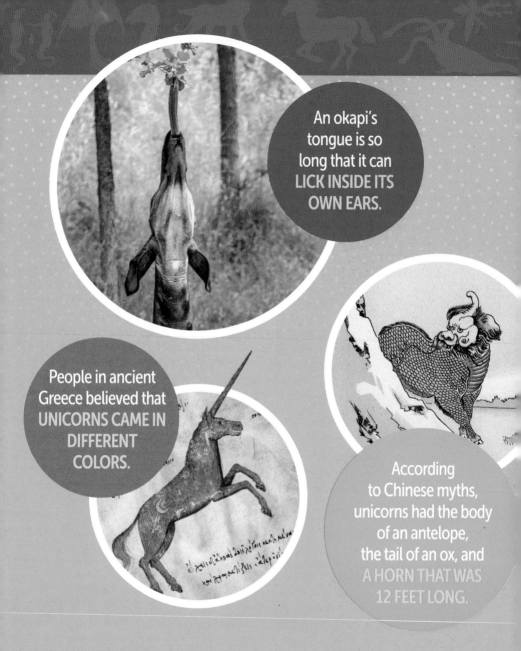

An okapi's tongue is so long that it can **LICK INSIDE ITS OWN EARS.**

People in ancient Greece believed that **UNICORNS CAME IN DIFFERENT COLORS.**

According to Chinese myths, unicorns had the body of an antelope, the tail of an ox, and A HORN THAT WAS 12 FEET LONG.

Their large ears alert them to even the slightest of sounds: When they sense danger coming, they hide. That means people rarely spot them. Until 1901, only local people knew about okapis!

In Peru, legend says that the dolphins that live in the Amazon River are SHAPE-SHIFTERS that TRANSFORM INTO HUMANS TO CAUSE MISCHIEF.

Planet Earth may not actually have shape-shifters, but real-life creatures do mimic other animals to play tricks.

The mimic octopus can CHANGE ITS SHAPE to look like other critters, including sea snakes, lionfish, and flatfish.

FROGFISH: These fish lie quietly on the seafloor, using their fins like hands to pull themselves forward. They wiggle a body part near their mouths that looks like a worm, shrimp, or other small sea creature. When a fish comes close to investigate— *CHOMP!*—the frogfish eats it.

SPICEBUSH SWALLOWTAIL CATERPILLARS: The young caterpillars are chocolate brown with white streaks, making them look like bird poo. As they grow up, they turn green and grow two spots that look like eyes. That makes them resemble a snake. Both of these forms keep other critters from eating them for lunch.

HOVERFLIES: These insects look just like honeybees—complete with yellow stripes and furry bodies! Like bees, hoverflies slurp up nectar from flowers. But unlike bees, hoverflies can't sting. Even so, their beelike appearance scares away predators.

According to English folklore, the boggart is an INVISIBLE BEAST that likes TO CAUSE MISCHIEF.

A glass frog's LARGE EYES help it see in the dark.

Invisible creatures don't exist. But see-through ones do! Reticulated glass frogs, which live in the rainforests of Central and South America, have transparent underbellies.

When this frog leaps from one leaf to another, it's possible to see some of its organs— even its beating heart! These frogs are small, about the length of a quarter. But they're fierce: Males will wrestle other frogs to protect their territory.

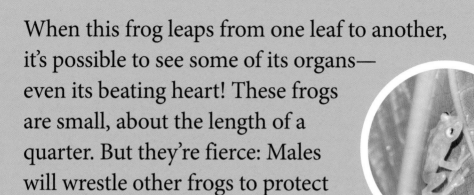

During the day, glass frogs CLING TO THE UNDERSIDE OF LEAVES to stay hidden.

The platypus is such a strange animal that the first scientists to see one thought someone was playing a trick on them. It looks like a mishmash of other animals.

Like the platypus, many creatures from Greek mythology were said to be a mix of animal parts. The most famous is the chimera (KIE-mir-ah), a monster that in one version of the tale has three heads: a lion's, a goat's, and a snake's.

The mythical monster Cerberus had THREE DOG HEADS, the claws of a lion, and the tail of a serpent.

Centaurs are HALF-HUMAN, HALF-HORSE CREATURES from Greek mythology.

According to one Native American legend, Pamola was a creature with the head of a MOOSE, the torso of a HUMAN, and the legs and wings of an EAGLE.

Most salamanders change from water-dwelling to land-living creatures as they reach adulthood. But AXOLOTLS don't: They keep their feathery gills their whole lives.

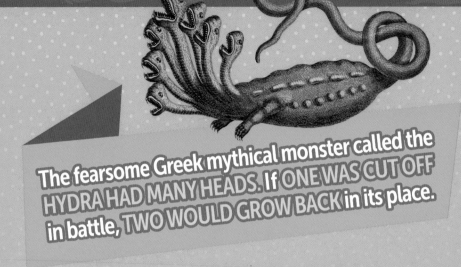

The fearsome Greek mythical monster called the HYDRA HAD MANY HEADS. If ONE WAS CUT OFF in battle, TWO WOULD GROW BACK in its place.

An axolotl (AX-uh-LAH-tul) is a salamander that lives in lakes and canals near Mexico City, Mexico. Like the mythical Hydra that can regrow its head, an axolotl can grow back a missing tail, an organ, and even part of its brain. Scientists are studying the axolotl to try to learn how it might be possible to someday regrow lost human limbs.

Ancient Aztec legends described the axolotl as A GOD IN DISGUISE.

a sculpture of the Aztec god Xolotl

Named After Legends

Though they're called VAMPIRE DEER, these animals use their fangs for fighting, not drinking blood.

Many kinds of male deer grow horns and antlers which they use to fight over females. But there's no room to swing those huge horns in the dense forests of Asia, where vampire deer live. Instead, they grow small, daggerlike tusks. That makes them look like vampires!

Other animals get their names from the legendary creatures they share a trait with, too.

According to myth, GARLIC KEEPS VAMPIRES AWAY.

vampire deer

These animals are so strange, they were named after mythical ones.

PINK FAIRY ARMADILLO: It doesn't cast magical spells ... but it does have a magical shell! This desert animal can pump blood in or out of its shell to cool down or warm up. Blood vessels under the shell give it a pink color.

A blue dragon's favorite food is the DEADLY PORTUGUESE MAN-OF-WAR, a creature similar to a jellyfish.

THORNY DEVIL: This critter looks fierce, thanks to the spines that cover its body. But it's only dangerous to ants—it uses its sticky tongue to eat 3,000 in a single meal.

Because of its **FURRY, WHITE** appearance, the **YETI CRAB** was named after the mythical creature of the Himalayan mountains.

BLUE DRAGON: This "dragon" is actually a tiny species of sea slug just about one inch long. They eat venomous creatures such as jellies, storing the stinging cells in their bodies. Then, if a predator tries to bite the sea slug, it gets a toxic mouthful!

CHAPTER 3

Mythical Powers

Orion the hunter was a GREEK MYTHOLOGICAL FIGURE with the ability to walk on water.

Walking on water is more than just a myth. Green basilisk lizards actually have this power! These unusual animals never stray far from water—because they use it to escape danger.

Basilisk lizards can RUN ACROSS WATER for 15 feet or more at a time.

They can also SWIM AND STAY UNDERWATER for 30 minutes.

When threatened, they can drop from the treetops to the water's surface and sprint right across! To do it, they unfurl fringes of skin on their toes. The skin traps pockets of air underneath their feet that keep them from sinking.

And these lizards are not the only real-life creatures with extraordinary powers.

Today, Orion is best known for the **CONSTELLATION NAMED IN HIS HONOR,** one of the most recognizable in the night sky.

The legendary phoenix could BURN UP IN FLAMES and be reborn OVER AND OVER AGAIN.

The mythical phoenix's supernatural power to be reborn seems like it could only be made up. But there is one real creature that shares this ability: the "immortal" jellyfish.

When it's young, it takes the form of a flower-like polyp. Later, the polyp transforms into an adult jelly. But when adult immortal jellyfish are faced with starvation or another danger, they can age in reverse, turning back into their polyp stage. From there, they can regrow into adults again and again!

phoenix

Tiny creatures called tardigrades can't live forever—but they can survive being BOILED, FROZEN, AND EXPOSED TO EXTREME PRESSURE AND RADIATION.

adult immortal jellyfish

Chameleons (kuh-MEEL-yuns) are real-life creatures with the power to transform their colors. Sometimes, like the mythical parandrus, they do it for camouflage (KAM-uh-flahj). They can blend in perfectly among leaves or branches.

Peacock flounder can CHANGE THEIR COLORS IN JUST EIGHT SECONDS.

But their most impressive color changes actually make them stand out. Male chameleons don't like to share their territory. When another male comes along, they will turn bold colors like yellow or red. The bright colors say "Back off!"

The whitebanded crab spider CHANGES COLOR TO MATCH THE FLOWERS IT HUNTS ON. It can attack its prey without being seen.

Mighty Defenses

The manticore was a terrifying mythical beast that could take down prey from a distance by shooting stingers from its tail. Other legendary creatures could breathe fire or snap with venomous fangs. But real-life animals have fierce defenses, too.

manticore

Here are five critters with abilities to match mythical monsters.

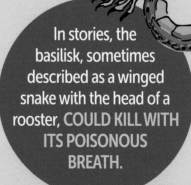

According to legend, anyone who looked into the eyes of the mythical Medusa WOULD BE TURNED TO STONE.

In stories, the basilisk, sometimes described as a winged snake with the head of a rooster, COULD KILL WITH ITS POISONOUS BREATH.

Blood squirting from its eyeballs!

HORNED LIZARD: Food is scarce in the desert. So, many animals, from coyotes to mice, will try to eat horned lizards. But they're in for a nasty surprise: This reptile can shoot bad-tasting blood ... from its eyes!

SHOCKING PINK DRAGON MILLIPEDE: This critter's bright pink color warns others: *Watch out!* If an attacker doesn't heed the warning, the shocking pink dragon millipede will blast it with a spray of toxic chemicals.

Bombardier beetles can ROTATE THEIR SPRAYER in nearly a complete circle to aim it at attackers.

BOMBARDIER BEETLE: When attacked, this beetle shoots super-heated sludge. It has two glands that release chemicals that combine to form a spray that's 212 degrees Fahrenheit, as hot as boiling water!

EXPLODING ANT: When one ant species from Borneo feels the colony is threatened, it will unleash an odd defense. The ant will turn its backside toward its attacker. Then it flexes its body until it explodes, releasing toxic yellow goo.

STRIPED POLECAT: It might look like a skunk, but the striped polecat is even stinkier! The fluid it sprays from glands under its tail smells so strong that this animal is often called the smelliest on Earth.

The striped polecat is ALSO CALLED A ZORILLA.

Planet Earth is packed with animals that have abilities that seem more like superpowers. Some are so impressive they were named after beasts found in legends. Others are so stunning that people of the past mistook them for mythical creatures.

They are not actually imaginary beasts. But hiding in every corner of our planet are animals so extraordinary, they seem that way!

Vampire bats RARELY BITE HUMANS, preferring cows, pigs, horses, and birds.

Vampires aren't real. But vampire bats really do drink blood.

1 Dragons are not real, but Komodo dragons are. At more than 300 pounds, they are the largest living lizards in the world.

2 In 2015, scientists named a newly discovered species of millipede after the jackal-headed Egyptian god Anubis.

3 Arachnids, which include spiders, were named after Arachne, a mythical weaver who was transformed into a spider.

4 "Zombie" ants are ants that have been infected with a fungus that takes over their brain and controls their movements.

5 Powerfully loud sperm whale calls can be louder than a jet engine.

6 In Greek mythology, satyrs were half-human and half-goat or half-horse creatures.

7 Draco, the mythical Roman dragon, could stun victims with its glowing skin. A lot of real animals glow, too, including fireflies and many deep-sea fish.

8 The star-nosed mole uses its powerful snout with 22 "tentacles" to find, catch, and eat food in less than a quarter of a second.

9 In Aztec mythology, Itzpapalotl (EETZ-pah-pah-low-tl) was a creature with jaguar-like claws whose name means "clawed butterfly." Butterflies really do have tiny claws that grasp branches and leaves.

10 Japanese folklore tells of a river monster called the Kappa. It may have been based on sightings of giant salamanders that grow up to five feet long.

11 Ancient people thought the giraffe was a creature called a "camelopard," a combination of a camel and a spotted leopard.

25 MORE FACTS

ABOUT MYTHICAL BEASTS AND UNBELIEVABLE REAL-LIFE CREATURES

12

Until the 20th century, some people believed that jackalopes—creatures like rabbits with horns—really existed.

13

Harpy eagles are named after half-woman, half-bird monsters in Greek mythology called harpies.

14

In ancient Egypt, sphinxes—creatures with the body of a lion and head of a human—were sometimes placed at the entrances of buildings to guard them.

15

In ancient Egypt and Greece, the ouroboros was a symbol of a legendary snake that eats its own tail, representing the circle of life.

16

The biggest living tarantula is the Goliath birdeater, which has a 12-inch leg span and is named after a biblical giant.

17

Goblin spiders have six eyes and live in the dirt—some even have horns. No wonder they're named after mythical monsters!

18

A prehistoric rhinoceros nicknamed the "Siberian unicorn" walked Earth about 40,000 years ago and was the size of an SUV.

19

Some species of "blind snakes" eat ants—just like amphisbaena (AM-fiss-bee-nah), a mythical serpent with a head at each end of its body.

20

The dinosaur *Sacisaurus* was named after a one-legged creature from Brazilian folklore because only right leg bones of the species have been found.

21

The ancient Roman author Pliny the Elder wrote about a mythical bull-like creature called the bonasus that sprayed its attackers with flaming hot dung.

22

Legend says the weasel is the only animal that can't be hurt by the mythical basilisk's venom. In reality, it's opossums that are immune to snake venom.

23

When ancient travelers saw a cotton plant for the first time, they thought it was actually an animal: a lamblike creature that grew tufts of wool.

24

Like Artemis, the Greek goddess of archery, archerfish shoot their insect prey. But instead of an arrow, they spit a stream of water into the air!

25

Though the Hydra was a mythical many-headed creature, two-headed turtles, snakes, and more can occasionally appear in nature.

Mythical Beasts Facts Roundup

WOW!
You flew through the tales of the most unbelievable creatures in history. Did you catch all 100 facts?

1. The Baku is a mythical Chinese and Japanese creature that eats dreams. 2. A mythical Aboriginal monster called the bunyip could have been inspired by the extinct *Diprotodon*. 3. The mythical Coyote character of Native American myths is smart and curious, like real coyotes. 4. Many ancient people thought unicorns were real animals. 5. Swift birds can fly without landing for 10 months straight. 6. The extinct *Titanoboa* was a real monster-size snake as long as a city bus. 7. Stories in ancient Greek mythology featured a giant monster with 100 hands. 8. In Arabic folklore, the Roc was a bird that could pick up and eat a human. 9. Horses inspired the mythical centaur, unicorn, and Pegasus. 10. Dolphins sleep with one eye open! 11. Wood frogs can survive being frozen in the winter. 12. Most hair samples that people claimed came from the mythical yeti actually came from bears. 13. When scientists discovered a 50-foot whale fossil, they named it Leviathan, after a biblical sea monster. 14. Myths of giant sea serpents might have been inspired by real-life giant oarfish. 15. In legends, the Mongolian death worm can kill its victims with electricity. 16. A real-life Bigfoot called *Gigantopithecus* existed until 100,000 years ago! 17. The mythical Nemean lion had a hide so tough no weapons could cut it. 18. The snapping shrimp sends out a jet of water at nearly 100 feet a second when it closes a claw. 19. Fenrir, a mythical Norse wolf, was so strong even the gods couldn't tame him. 20. The ancient Greeks believed that creatures called sirens could trick sailors into crashing their ships. 21. Some people think the legendary Loch Ness monster is a plesiosaur—a reptile that went extinct about 66 million years ago. 22. The mythical Greek monster called the Minotaur had the body of a human and the head and tail of a bull. 23. In ancient Egypt, cats were thought to be magical creatures that could bring good luck. 24. Lenape and Iroquois legends tell that the world was created on the back of a giant sea turtle. 25. According to Chinese myth, the animals of the world raced to see which 12 would become the symbols of the zodiac. 26. Queen Elizabeth I paid £10,000 for what she thought was a unicorn's horn covered with jewels. 27. A narwhal's tusk can be nearly nine feet long. 28. Scientists aren't sure what narwhals use their tusks for. 29. The narwhal's tusk is a tooth that grows out of its upper lip. 30. In 1608, Henry Hudson wrote that his crew saw a creature with the body of a woman and the tail of a porpoise. 31. Manatees are distantly related to elephants. 32. A manatee relative is the dugong, which gets its name from the Malay word for "lady of the sea." 33. In 1853, an enormous creature with long tentacles was found on a beach in Denmark. It looked like a sea monster! 34. Giant squid have three hearts. 35. Giant squid have eyes the size of dinner plates. 36. "Cyclops" means "round eye." 37. The legendary rainbow serpent was an immortal creature with a multicolored body. 38. Some nudibranchs fend off predators with stingers and toxic goo. 39. Nudibranchs are picky eaters—some eat only one kind of prey. 40. The horselike okapi is so hard to find in the wild that it was once thought to be a unicorn. 41. An okapi's

tongue is so long that it can lick inside its own ears. 42. People in ancient Greece believed that unicorns came in different colors. 43. According to Chinese myths, unicorns had the body of an antelope, the tail of an ox, and a horn that was 12 feet long. 44. In Peru, legend says that Amazon river dolphins are shape-shifters. 45. The mimic octopus can change its shape to look like other critters. 46. Some frogfish can change color to blend in with sponges or coral around them. 47. Spicebush swallowtail caterpillars roll leaves around their bodies to hide from predators. 48. According to English folklore, the boggart is an invisible beast that causes mischief. 49. A glass frog's large eyes help it see in the dark. 50. Glass frogs cling to the underside of leaves to stay hidden. 51. A platypus has webbed feet and a bill like a duck's, a tail like a beaver's, and a body like an otter's. 52. The mythical monster Cerberus had three dog heads, the claws of a lion, and the tail of a serpent. 53. Centaurs are half-human, half-horse creatures from Greek mythology. 54. According to one legend, Pamola had the head of a moose, the torso of a human, and the legs and wings of an eagle. 55. Unlike most salamanders, axolotls don't change from water-dwelling to land-living as they reach adulthood. They keep their gills. 56. The Greek mythical monster called the Hydra had many heads. 57. Ancient Aztec legends described the axolotl as a god in disguise. 58. "Vampire deer" use their fangs for fighting, not drinking blood. 59. According to myth, garlic keeps vampires away. 60. A blue dragon's favorite food is the deadly Portuguese man-of-war. 61. The yeti crab was named after the mythical creature of the Himalayan mountains. 62. Orion, the Greek mythological figure, could walk on water. 63. Basilisk lizards can run across water. 64. They can also swim and stay underwater for 30 minutes. 65. Today, Orion is best known for the constellation named in his honor. 66. The legendary phoenix could burn up in flames and be reborn again and again. 67. Tiny tardigrades can survive being boiled, frozen, and exposed to extreme pressure and radiation. 68. The parandrus is a mythical beast that could change its color to hide in its surroundings. 69. Peacock flounder can change their colors in just eight seconds. 70. The whitebanded crab spider changes color to match the flowers it hunts on. 71. Legend says anyone who looked into mythical Medusa's eyes would be turned to stone. 72. In stories, the basilisk could kill with its venomous breath. 73. Bombardier beetles can rotate their sprayer in nearly a complete circle to aim it at attackers. 74. The striped polecat is also called a zorilla. 75. Vampire bats rarely bite humans. 76. Komodo dragons are more than 300 pounds and the largest living lizards. 77. Scientists named a species of millipede after the Egyptian god Anubis. 78. Arachnids were named after Arachne, a mythical weaver who was transformed into a spider. 79. "Zombie" ants have been infected with a fungus that takes over their brains and controls their movements. 80. Sperm whale calls can be louder than a jet engine. 81. In Greek mythology, satyrs were half-human and half-goat or half-horse creatures. 82. Draco, the mythical Roman dragon, could stun victims with its glowing skin. 83. The star-nosed mole uses its snout with 22 "tentacles" to find, catch, and eat food. 84. In Aztec mythology, the creature Itzpapalotl's name means "clawed butterfly." 85. Japanese folklore tells of a river monster called the Kappa. 86. Ancient people thought the giraffe was a "camelopard," a combination of a camel and a spotted leopard. 87. Until the 20th century, some people believed that jackalopes really existed. 88. Harpy eagles are named after half-woman, half-bird monsters in Greek mythology called harpies. 89. In ancient Egypt, sphinxes were sometimes placed at building entrances to guard them. 90. In ancient Egypt and Greece, the ouroboros was a symbol of a legendary snake that eats its own tail. 91. The biggest tarantula is the Goliath birdeater, named after a biblical giant. 92. Goblin spiders have six eyes and live in dirt—some even have horns. 93. A prehistoric rhinoceros, the "Siberian unicorn," was the size of an SUV. 94. Some species of "blind snakes" eat ants—just like amphisbaena, a mythical serpent. 95. The dinosaur *Sacisaurus* was named after a one-legged creature from Brazilian folklore. 96. Ancient author Pliny the Elder described the mythical bonasus that sprayed its attackers with hot dung. 97. Legend says the weasel can't be hurt by the mythical basilisk's venom. 98. Ancient travelers thought the cotton plant was an animal: a lamblike creature that grew tufts of wool. 99. Archerfish spit a stream of water into the air to shoot their insect prey. 100. Two-headed turtles, snakes, and more can occasionally appear in nature.

INDEX

Boldface indicates illustrations.